Integral Mission:

THE M-SERIES are a collection of short, accessible papers and articles from Micah Global, being developed in response to the need for clear, authoritative statements on key themes. They form a foundation of historical and current ideas that contribute to our understanding and practice of integral mission. They aim to promote reflection, dialogue, articulation and action on the major concepts and issues that move us towards transforming mission.

The M-series are an essential resource for practitioners, theologians, students, leaders, and teachers.

M-Series from im:press

Titles in print:

Integral Mission: Biblical foundations
by Melba Maggay

The Five Marks of Mission:
Making God's mission ours by Chris Wright

In preparation:

Towards Transformed Honour by Arley Loewen

Paying the Unpaid Debts by Flip Buys

Integral Mission:
Biblical foundations

Melba Padilla Maggay
Chairperson, ISACC Philippines
President, Micah Global

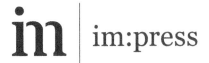

First published by ISACC, Philippines

Copyright © Institute for Studies in Asian Church and Culture, 2007

Reproduced by permission

The author asserts the moral right
to be identified as the author of this work

Published by

im:press

An imprint of Micah Global

ISBN: 978-0-9945911-2-8

Typeset in Warnock Pro

Printed and bound by Ingram Spark

One

Integral Mission:
what's it all about?

FOR about three decades now there has been a growing recognition, especially in the global South, that the mission of the church is more than just 'saving souls.' In many poor countries, the sharp increase in poverty has forced a rethinking of what the church must be doing. There is the practical pressure of having to face up to the realities of hardship. There is the alarming sense that the usual structures and ways of 'being church' no longer work.

The dizzying pace of technological innovations has made most of us feel overwhelmed, if not incompetent. We now live in a world where the old certainties are not so much challenged as bypassed. The old wineskins in which we have understood and proclaimed the gospel are fast getting obsolete.

Timelessness and universality are in the nature of our faith; the gospel is always new wine, speaking to all times and all cultures. Unfortunately, its wineskins—those structures and established norms by which we live and proclaim it—are always getting old.

The media prophet Marshall McLuhan once said, "If anything works, it's obsolete." Bible translations that have served generations, like the King James Version, with its magnificent cadence and resonances, had to be retired. Cherished hymns, creeds and prayers, no matter how well-loved, soon get out of date to the modern ear. Accepted ways of doing evangelism and mission, mostly framed within Western contexts, no longer work in a multicultural world.

This is also why church growth theories come and go. For a while, people may behave in certain predictable social patterns. But these are at best snapshots of moving pictures. Cultures change and societies adapt to new structures. This constant flux and impermanence is described in haunting words by Isaiah: "All flesh is grass, and all its beauty is like the flower of the field; the grass withers, and the flower falls ..." (Isaiah 40:6) The things of earth are transient; we all decay, die and disintegrate.

Today, we are hearing a call to a fresh understanding of what it means to follow Jesus in our world. There was a time when this was understood merely as 'receiving Jesus as personal Lord and Saviour,' by which is meant that we secure a ticket to heaven by repenting of our sins (the 'saviour' part), and being subject to him in our lives (the 'lordship' part). Discipleship is understood as mostly, and often solely, spiritual and personal: going to church, evangelizing, doing other such religious activities, coupled with clean living and staying away from vices. While all this has value in itself, the call to follow Jesus is deeper than getting religious, wider than being released from guilt, and broader than trying to be good peaceable citizens who pay taxes and stay away from getting into trouble with the powers.

> *Today, we are hearing a call to a fresh understanding of what it means to follow Jesus in our world*

The mission to which Jesus calls us has been framed in recent decades in terms of the relationship of evangelism and social action, or the need for both 'proclamation' and 'presence.' As the Lausanne Covenant of 1974 puts it, "We affirm that evangelism and socio-political involvement are both part of our Christian duty." However, the Covenant maintains that since evangelism is eternal in its consequences, it has priority over social involvement. While this is progress from the old pietism, it reflects a certain habit of mind still rooted in Greek dualism, expressed in such polarities as the scholastic dichotomy between 'nature' and 'grace', or between the 'sacred' and the 'secular'.

In contrast, the work of Jesus has a breadth and a wholeness that is lacking in our usual grasp of what his mission is about. We are told that he died, not just for the forgiveness of sins, but for the redeeming of the entire creation, to reconcile to himself all things, whether things on earth or things in heaven, and bring all things together under him.

> *Jesus stopped to attend to a trembling woman's need, a delay that must have been agony to a man waiting for him to heal a sick child*

The work of Christ on the cross has far-reaching social and cosmic consequences (Romans 8:19-22, Colossians 1:20, Ephesians 1:9-10).

Likewise, his life had a seamlessness that honoured the humdrum humbleness of ordinary things, even as he was engaged in a deadly struggle with the powers. He took time to party, to play with children, to sit and talk to a woman at a well about water that can quench her deepest thirst. On his way to heal an important man's dying child, he sensed that someone had touched him, not in the way that a crowd presses, but in a desperate reaching out, such that power had gone forth from him. He stopped to attend to a trembling woman's need, a delay that must have been agony to a man waiting for him to heal a sick child that was about to die (Luke 8:40-56).

Jesus never went past a needy man or woman just because he had to be going. He had this unerring instinct that all that comes his way is part of the mission that God had given to him.

In both the life and teaching of Jesus, there is not this tediously calculating bent towards asking what is priority or which has eternal significance. To him, the giving of a cup of water can be just as spiritual as the casting out of demons. A small gesture, it will by no means lose its reward at the end of time if consciously done in honour of his name (Mark 9: 38-41). All of life, when lived and offered up to him, becomes a living sacrifice, an act of worship and witness to the fact that "the earth is the Lord's, and everything in it." (Romans 12:1, Psalm 24:1)

This sense of life as whole and seamless we are to imitate, for "As the Father has sent me, so I send you." (John 20:21) We get a clear picture of what this means when Jesus sent out the twelve disciples. At the core of his instructions was a two-fold mission: "As you go, preach this message: 'The kingdom of heaven is near.' Heal the sick, raise the dead, cleanse those who have leprosy, drive out demons." (Matthew 10:7-8)

> *The proclamation that the King has come is to be accompanied by visible signs of the presence of his kingdom*

Notice that the mission of the twelve had both a verbal and a nonverbal dimension. They were to announce that the kingdom is near, and authenticate its presence by demonstrating its powers. They were to bear the good news as well as the reality of the new social order: health for the sick, life for the dead, cleansing for those declared ritually unclean, light to those who sit in the shadows, and deliverance from oppression and spiritual torment. The proclamation that the King has come, that he has disarmed the usurper and now rules over all of humankind, is to be accompanied by visible signs of the presence of his kingdom.

In this light, there is no point to the controversy between those who preach the gospel and say it is sufficient, 'for it is the power of God unto salvation', and those who heal and do works of mercy and say these are good and are witness in themselves. Word and works are meant to be together.

We propose that we frame all that we do and say within the broader compass of what the Bible calls 'witness'. Works of justice and mercy are part of our witness, but are not to be confused with evangelism, for *evangelizomai* in the original Greek has a distinctly 'chattering' or verbal meaning. Similarly, evangelism may transform individuals and foster righteousness, but it cannot substitute for actual confrontation with the forces that create poverty and injustice. Change in individuals does not necessarily mean change in society. There are far more complex forces at work that require engagement at ground level by those specifically called to bring their expertise and giftedness to bear in the political arena.

> *Change in individuals does not necessarily mean change in society*

Ultimately, for the Word to make sense, it needs a caring community, a social context in which the saving power of God takes flesh and is made visible. Likewise, our acts of mercy and compassion need articulating within the interpretive frame of the gospel if they are to be bearers of the meaning of the kingdom and not just another instance of competent social work.

This 'show-and-tell' nature of our mission brings out the principle that non-verbal messages constitute as much as 70% of what we communicate; the verbal part is only 30%. This means that what people see is just as important as what people hear. In fact, we are told that when verbal and non-verbal signals conflict, people tend to believe the non-verbal. The credibility of what we say is compromised by the lack of consistency with what we do. When our words do not lead to authentic deeds, they are only words and lose power. It is this gap between word and deed which accounts for much of the powerlessness of our witness today.

Integral mission involves saying, doing and being people in the Kingdom. It should be understood as having to do not only with evangelism and social action, but with all of what it means to bear witness to the reign of Jesus in all of life. It means sexual purity, keeping our marriages and families intact, and in general widening the political space for ethical choices that are consistent with the Christian tradition. But it also means defending the human rights of all peoples, respecting their cultural practices and religious convictions within the limits and civilities of a pluralistic society.

It means forgiveness for people tortured by guilt, and reconciliation for societies wracked by conflict. It bids us to feed the poor and make sure that power structures are just. It means waging spiritual warfare in the heavenly realms, but also destroying strongholds in the mind. We make every thought captive to obey Christ, engaging the intellectual life and the systems and patterns of our culture (2 Corinthians 10:4-5).

We are pilgrims looking forward to an altogether new world, yet also inheritors of this earth, re-creating and conforming it to the image of the Son. We affirm all that is true and lovely and just around us, supporting governance, creating art, inventing technologies that honour the Creator. But we also hold accountable those who have power over us, resisting the Beast and critiquing the myths and stories constructed for us by media or the 'prince of the power of the air' in our time (Philippians 4:8, Romans 13:1-7, Genesis 4:19-22, John 18:22-23, Acts 16:35-40, Revelation 13, Ephesians 2:2).

> *We are pilgrims looking forward to an altogether new world, yet also inheritors of this earth*

Such is the height, the length and the breadth of the mission to which God calls us. it requires the gifts and the resources of the whole Church.

To those specifically called to the ministry of helping and speaking up for the poor, this definition of integral mission from the Micah Network Declaration sums it up with great clarity. It sums up what it is about to the 140 leaders of mission and development organizations who signed it at a consultation held in Oxford in 2001:

> Integral mission or holistic transformation is the proclamation and demonstration of the gospel. It is not simply that evangelism and social involvement are to be done alongside each other. Rather, in integral mission our proclamation has social consequences as we call people to love and repentance in all areas of life. And our social involvement has evangelistic consequences as we bear witness to the transforming grace of Jesus Christ. If we ignore the world we betray the word of God which sends us out to serve the world. If we ignore the word of God we have nothing to bring to the world. Justice and justification by faith, worship and political action, the spiritual and the material, personal change and structural change belong together. As in the life of Jesus, being, doing and saying are at the heart of our integral task.

Two

What does the Lord require of us?

Introduction

THE recurrent political crisis of the Philippines is not going to be solved by the usual tools of change. As with much of our life these days, we are stumped, baffled by all the technological changes around us, and by the persistence of ancient wrongs that do not yield to all our efforts at social engineering. The paradigms which frame our understanding of our social problems are hopelessly outdated and obsolete. In times like this we are tempted to throw up our hands, avert our eyes and look for somewhere else—preferably the USA—where we can find decent jobs, hole up and live our lives in peace.

But as people of God, what does the Lord require of us in a time such as this?

This question is not unlike the question playing in the minds of the people of Israel in a time when they thought they had turned back to God and were quite punctilious in performing their religious duties. It was a time when ritual purity had been restored in the worship of Yahweh; 'so what else does God want from us'? We are given a pointed answer by the prophet Micah, the last of the four great prophets of the eighth century before Christ.

On doing justice and kindness: Micah 6:1-8

This passage begins with a court scene, a cosmic legal drama where God as plaintiff puts forward his case against Israel as defendant. Yahweh summons the hills, the mountains and the very foundations of the earth to hear his case and stand as silent witnesses (6:1-2).

"What have I done to you?" was the Lord's anguished cry. "How have I burdened you?" Far from wearying Israel, Yahweh recounts his mighty saving acts on behalf of his people, beginning with Exodus and on to the conquest of the promised land. Accompanying them on their journey, he provided them with able leadership, protected them from harm, blessed and fought with them all the way to the land beyond the Jordan (6:3-5).

But once settled, Israel quickly became unfaithful, rife with injustice and oppression. This social disorder existed alongside a resuscitated religiosity. Prophetic warnings of a coming judgment—the fall of Judah—were parried by a misplaced confidence in Jerusalem and its temple as declared centre of God's presence (3:11-12).

With this as social backdrop, Micah prophesies against a religion that does not lead the faithful to actual practice of justice and righteousness.

The case against Israel

Micah prophesied in a time just like ours. There was, if you like, what we would call a 'revival.' King Hezekiah had removed the idolatrous altars from the hills and mountain tops of the country, and great religious reforms were taking place. Yet this ritual purity and resurgence of religiosity had not affected the way they did business, nor the social structures of their day.

The aristocracy ruled corruptly. They seized, by force and fraud, the lands and houses of small landowners. The magnates bribed the courts, business reeked with dishonesty. Prophets and priests were mercenaries, using religion to silence the voice of the oppressed and justify the violence of

This ritual purity and resurgence of religiosity had not affected the way they did business

the rich. They lulled the people into a false hope, confident that Jerusalem—and the temple in it—will always stand: "Is not the Lord among us? No disaster will come upon us." All around was violence, deceit and the breakdown of trust even within families and friendships. (Micah 2:1-2; 3:1-11; 6:9-12; 7:2-6)

Against this terrible social landscape, the people of Israel, appallingly clueless, did not quite get what the Lord was railing about. Against a backdrop of patent injustice, all that the people of Israel could think of was that they might have been remiss in their ritual duties. They thought that more religion was the answer.

Does God need more religion?
"With what shall I come before the Lord, and bow down before the exalted God?"

Here, Micah puts to words Israel's understanding of what the Lord must be asking from them. We sense a certain punctiliousness in keeping the laws of the sacrificial system: "Shall I come before him with burnt offerings, with calves a year old?" The notion that God could be appeased by extravagant offerings surfaces in this rhetorical hyperbole: "Will the Lord be pleased with thousands of rams, with ten thousand rivers of oil?"

Such earnest religiosity and lavish cultic devotion did not seem to be enough. There was the willingness to sacrifice even a precious firstborn son: "Shall I offer my firstborn for my transgression, the fruit of my body for the sin of my soul?" The stern asceticism behind this horrible exchange is undoubtedly an influence of the nations round about them. Child sacrifice was expressly forbidden in the Mosaic law. That this thing can be found in Israel is indication of a creeping paganism: of how the people, bereft of insight, have slowly absorbed the cultures of their neighbours.

What the Lord requires
In response to Israel's question, Micah, with his peasant bluntness, was forthright: "He has showed you, O man, what is good. And what does

the Lord require of you, but to do justice, to love kindness, and to walk humbly with your God?" (Micah 6:8 RSV) This text is perhaps the most famous and the high point of Micah's teaching. It summarizes the messages of the great prophets of the eighth century: Amos on righteousness, Hosea on steadfast love, and Isaiah on faith and obedience.

Instead of more religion, the Lord requires, first and foremost, the doing of justice. It is worth noting that in the Old Testament, 'justice' and 'righteousness' are used interchangeably. To 'do justice' is to 'declare one right' (2 Samuel 15:4, Psalm 82:3, Exodus 23:6-8). Justice is mentioned 26 times in the Old Testament, once as a translation of the Hebrew *mispat*, as in this passage, but more often of the word *sedeq* or *sedeqa*, 'righteousness'. When these Hebrew words appear together, they are usually translated as 'justice and righteousness', as in the prophet Amos' ringing declaration: "... let justice roll on like a river, righteousness like a never-failing stream." (Amos 5:24) Justice and righteousness are usually treated as a pair, understood as one unit of thought.

> There is no divorce between concern for justice and personal righteousness, social liberation and loving acts of mercy

What this means is that there is no biblical warrant for the kind of divide we see in our day between those who espouse 'moral' issues like abortion, divorce or homosexuality, and those concerned for 'political' issues like land reform or global fair trade. Unlike the culture wars in the US and in other places, where conservatives tend to put emphasis on 'righteousness' or moral issues, and liberals on 'justice' or social issues, the Bible puts these two together as our twin mandate. There is no divorce between concern for justice and personal righteousness, governance and giving, social liberation and loving acts of mercy.

Together with justice, we are to love kindness, or, in the more modern translations, mercy. We are told by scholars that the Hebrew *hesed* refers to a steadfast love that binds two parties in a covenant. Besides kindness, it connotes loyalty and solidarity, as against the tendency these days to disavow responsibility for one another. It describes a kind of social contract where those at the edges of society are especially cared for. This is a stark contrast to the hardness we see today, where there is a return to the 'survival of the fittest', a kind of social Darwinism where the weak and the poor are sidelined, left to adapt and fend for themselves within the hard and abstract mechanisms of market forces.

A theologian once defined mercy as "the coming down of the Almighty to rescue the needy". This is power on the side of the powerless. It is effective compassion focused on those who cannot defend themselves against forces that put them down and make sink deeper and deeper into misery.

> *God alone is worthy of all that we work and long for, all that we have and all that we are*

Alongside the concern for justice and mutual caring is walking humbly with God. Without God as our centre, we get deluded by a Messiah complex. We get this disproportionate sense that our work is so important that we should sacrifice everything to the altar of the cause we serve. It becomes an idol, such that we become hard-nosed knights of justice, sacrificing people to the abstract symmetry of an idea.

Merely humanist ideologies lead to 'killing fields', whether those of Stalinist Russia or Pol Pot's Cambodia, or our own mass graves of New People's Army revolutionaries executed by their former comrades. We need a deeper, higher reason for why we live and die. God alone is worthy of all that we work and long for, all that we have and all that we are. Without God, we reduce people into abstract statistics that have value only as part of a collective. Or we make ourselves into supermen, like Ayn Rand's mythical Atlas, carrying within ourselves the fiction that the world moves because of us. God's presence in our lives gives us a sense of proportion. We are neither too small nor too big. It is a corrective against hubris, that overweening sense that we are 'free and to none accountable,' as one of Milton's demonic characters puts it.

Walking with God also means that we are ever conscious of where our power lies. After three decades of social activism, I have become aware that all change begins from the inside. It begins in that place where the Spirit moves people from helplessness to a sense of power, from despair to hope. It is a place where none of us can go. The best that we can do is to watch and wait for

> *We are to love kindness, to embody in our personal lives God's passionate particularity over those who are swept to the edges of life*

those faint stirrings within when the poor discover who and what they are, and begin to have a sense of the possible such that they take their life in their own hands.

Walking with God means that we live close enough to him that we hear the thud of his footfall in human history. Often, we miss our historical cues because we get hard of hearing. We are not able to discern those *kairos* moments when God summons us to rise to the call of the kingdom and make its presence felt in the halls of the great.

These, then, are what the Lord requires. We are to act justly, to see to it that the structures of our society are fair to those who are powerless and voiceless. We are to love kindness, to embody in our personal lives God's passionate particularity over those who are swept to the edges of life. We are to combine appreciation of the complex social forces behind poverty with a certain simplicity about our responsibility to care for the concrete needs of those around us. We cannot be like Lucy, that smart but crabby girl in the cartoon Peanuts, who says "I love humanity ... it's people I hate."

Most of all, we walk with God, who is the source of all life and meaning. Without him, we become mere activists who degenerate into judge and executioner of those who don't happen to fit our ideal social order. Or we become mere social workers, an army of 'bleeding hearts' who get burnt out by do-gooding. Again and again, we need to ask: "Where does the power come from?" Is the force coming from a hard drivenness to get things done? Or is our work borne by the Spirit's gentle wind beneath our wings?

True religion, says Micah, always has social consequences. God is not as interested in sacrifices as in just governance and right dealings in the marketplace. He also cares for what we do with the need of our neighbours, those around us who daily call on our compassion. We are told that the poor, quite mysteriously, are proxies for Jesus. Whatever kindness we do to the least of these, we do to Christ. Love for Jesus cannot be separated from love of neighbour.

Ultimately, if we truly love God, we will work for justice and show kindness to the needy. Knowing that we cannot do these without him, we walk closely with him and humbly seek his face for our daily sustenance. Mother Teresa once remarked before journalists that people have a mistaken notion about the work of the Sisters of Charity. "We do this for Jesus," she said. What enables them, day in and day out, to care for the needy is this spiritual centre where they get fed by the grace and presence of Christ. In the face of so much suffering and urgent need, they sustain themselves by maintaining a liturgical centre, returning again and again to the ultimate reason for which they accompany the sorrowing and the dying. Such work, after all, is but part of their seamless walk with God.

Three

The Greatest Commandment

Introduction

To LOVE GOD, says Jesus, is very like loving our neighbour. What does this mean?

First, it means to turn from the idols of our time and bring our lives and central structures—like family and governance—under his lordship.

It means naming and dethroning the powers that rule our lives, our cultures and our life systems. For churches in the West, it may mean not just turning away from materialism, but confronting the forces that make the rest of the world poor. For those of us in the global South, it may mean breaking free, not just from the stranglehold of ancestral and nature spirits, but from hierarchies, authorities and systems that keep people poor, oppressed and without rights.

On an individual level, we have to ensure that all we do really proceeds from the love of God. Often, there is a great deal of stress and anxiety in those who care for the needy among us. It may be that our lifeline to God has dried up, and we have ceased to drink deeply of the only well that sustains life, health and passion. It

> *Often, there is a great deal of stress and anxiety in those who care for the needy among us*

may be that we "have hewn out cisterns for yourselves, broken cisterns that can hold no water" as Jeremiah puts it. Like Israel, we trust in the jars of clay that our hands have fashioned, only to discover, in the heat and drought of summer, that the water has seeped through the cracks, lapped dry by the parched ground.

One sign that our hearts are going astray is when the daily battle against the evils of poverty and injustice begins to erode our own inner spirit. We lose confidence in the quiet efficacy of the kingdom to change our societies. Our idealism quickly turns into cynicism, and the experience of failure drives us to show some success in the difficult work that we do. Sooner or later, it is this drivenness, and not the call and love of God, that fuels the things we do.

> There is no sense in which we can love God without at the same time loving our neighbour

Now and again, we need to ask, "where does the power come from?" If it is not from God, it is coming from some other source, some powerful idol that has begun to grip our soul.

Secondly, loving God and loving our neighbour is a single, not a sequential act. It is not that when we love God, we shall, in the next instance, love others also. Jesus makes the two commandments virtually one, such that there is no sense in which we can love God without at the same time loving our neighbour.

Scripture elsewhere illustrates how this works. Matthew 25:40 tells us that the poor, in a very real yet mysterious sense, are 'proxies for Christ', to borrow the phrase of the Jesuit Aloysius Pieris. Part of the mystery of the incarnate God is that he has so identified with those in the margins, that their hunger, nakedness and strangeness have become his. What we do with the poor, we do with Jesus.

James strongly picks up this theme by refusing the divide between word and deed, faith and works, or, in contemporary language, religion and social action. "Religion that God our Father accepts as pure and faultless is this: to look after orphans and widows in their distress and to keep oneself from being polluted by the world." (James 1:26-27) In this, James echoes the Old Testament concern for the poor, the widow, the orphan and the sojourner, those who are swept to the margins and are rendered vulnerable because of scarce resources, outright lack of means for survival, or not having the right ethnicity or nationality. True religion always has social and moral consequences.

Conversely, we cannot truly love our neighbour without at the same time loving God. There is no force on earth, besides the grace of God, that can deliver us from the insatiable appetite for profit, or the many subtle ways by which we use 'the greater good for the greater number' to camouflage our interests and eliminate competition or opposition. Biblical pessimism about human nature tells us that no amount of social engineering can neutralize the acquisitive instinct and will to power, or reorder the sinful bent towards selfishness and greed.

Also, failed communist experiments have shown us that without subjection to God, our social projects send people to their destruction: witness the 'killing fields' of Cambodia, or that vast Soviet labyrinth of despair called the Gulag Archipelago. The Russian novelist Fyodor Dostoyevsky, writing in the 19th century, predicted that "with the downfall of the altar of God, we are left with either the superman or the anthill." Without the high and humbling view that we are made in the image of a great God, we lose a sense of proportion about ourselves. We either elevate ourselves to the status of a superman to whom 'everything is permitted', as Raskolnikov in *Crime and Punishment* puts it, or we get reduced to an army of automatons who have value only as part of a grand collective. We then play god and treat others who get in our way as insects to be exterminated.

> *To love God is to love beyond boundaries, be it of race or of notions of purity or uncleanness*

Thirdly, to love God is to love beyond boundaries, be it of race or of notions of purity or uncleanness. This is the pointed message of the parable of the Good Samaritan. (Luke 10:25-37) The 'expert in the law' was taken aback by Jesus' backhanded charge that he put to practice what he well knew to be the way to life. Instead of applying to himself the meaning of loving God and neighbour, he engaged Jesus on an abstract discussion of a technical detail: "And who is my neighbour?"

Jesus refused to get drawn into the finer points of this theoretical question. He told the story of how a member of a despised race—the Samaritans—proved to be more of a neighbour to someone in need than the religious leaders of his day. Both the priest and the Levite "passed by on the other side," perhaps to avoid having to touch what looked like a dead body. Apparently, fear of ritual contamination took prior importance to helping the man, in contrast to the Samaritan, who was simply moved to pity and took all the trouble and expense needed to take care of him.

> *What we do with the poor among us is a test of what we are as a society and as a people of God*

Jesus then asked, "Which of these three do you think was a neighbour to the man who fell into the hands of robbers?" Thus he shifted the issue from "who has the right to be called my neighbour?" to "who has actively served as neighbour?" To Jesus, it is not important who or what kind of people should get help—they could be morally unsavoury characters like prostitutes, traitors like tax collectors, or Gentiles like the Widow at Zarephath. The more relevant question is, "who is prepared to be neighbour to anyone in need?" Jesus shows up false religion here, and radically breaks down fences, refusing barriers of race, religious scruples and pieties in the face of someone's need for compassion.

To conclude: Since loving God and loving our neighbour is a single act, what we do with the poor among us is a test of what we are as a society and as a people of God.

This linking together of love of God and love of neighbour is what gives sacramental value and eternal significance to our small gestures of compassion. It is what makes work such as that of Mother Theresa among the sick and the dying in the streets of Calcutta a compelling sign of the presence of Christ. As she disclaimed once in an interview: "We are not social workers," she said, correcting mistaken notions that this is all being done for merely humanitarian reasons. No, she said, " ... we do this for the love of Jesus."

Ultimately, it is the love of God and neighbour that will make any work endure.

Serving the poor: Some issues

A liberating compassion. In responding to the needy, the church has tended to put emphasis either on social compassion or social construction. The pendulum tends to swing between purely personal involvement or structural engagement, depending on such factors as to whether the church is in a minority or majority situation, theologically tending to withdraw because it is pessimistic about the world or confidently engaged because the Kingdom is now at work in the world.

Historically, the Jews were told to create a society where, because of the memory of their own slavery, the poor, the weak and the stranger are to be treated with special care. There were gleaning and harvest laws meant to provide for landless poor like Ruth and Naomi. (Exodus 23:10-11, Leviticus 19:9-10, Ruth 2) There were legal safeguards against taking advantage of those who are especially vulnerable, like the widow, orphan and the alien in their midst. (Exodus 22:21-24). Their internal economy forbids lending to the needy with interest. The poor debtor must be treated with courtesy, and his collateral, like the cloak that he uses against the cold, must be returned by sunset. (Exodus 22:25-27, Deuteronomy 24:10-13) These are but some of the host of legislation designed to 'remember the poor'. In both the Old and New Testament, there is strong concern that Israel should put them at the centre of their vision. (See, for instance, Deuteronomy 14:28-29, 15:7, 24:14-15, Psalm 41:1, Proverbs 19:17, Matthew 19:21, Galatians 2:10) .

The early Church built on Judaism's legacy of institutionalized charity. They pooled their resources together, enrolled widows into some kind of feeding program, and in general functioned as a social safety net for those who are especially needing help among them (Acts 2:43-44, 5:1-11, 6:1-7).

Missionary movements, like the modern ones that rose from the evangelical awakenings of the 18th century onwards, likewise built schools and hospitals in their wake, doing various works of mercy in far-flung places alongside evangelization. The impact of such work can be seen in the likes of Nelson Mandela, who in the 1998 world assembly of the World Council of Churches in Harare paid tribute to such efforts. As a boy he was too poor, he said. If it were not for the mission schools, he could not have gone to school.

Such institutions of social compassion are important in themselves and have their own value and integrity. They are not to be treated as mere means to an end, like evangelism or some such enterprise.

> We need to engage in politics, recompose power elites and do advocacy on behalf of those who cannot speak for themselves

At the same time, it is important to grasp that mere social development can run into a bottomless pit. Development experiences in Africa and other places show that incessant political conflicts, tribal wars, bad governance and other such systemic ills result in unsettled demographics and perpetual instability. Painstaking development gains in grassroots communities can get easily wiped out by political disasters.

Confronting power structures. People of faith have shown themselves to be fairly good in concrete delivery of social services. The presence of a volunteer force, dedicated staff, and relatively high standards of professional and ethical commitment are today enabling many faith-based organizations to win the trust and respect of donor communities. There is need, however, to address the larger context of poverty and injustice. Besides relief and development, we need to engage in politics, recompose power elites, restructure social arrangements and do various advocacies on behalf of those who cannot speak for themselves (Proverbs 31:8-9).

There is the idea among us that evangelism is in itself a response to the need for social transformation. Changing individuals will automatically mean change in societies. This is not always true. Often, there are larger, much more complex forces at work that keep people in bondage to poverty in many societies. We are not just battling against flesh and blood, but against "the rulers, against the authorities, against the powers of this dark world and against the spiritual forces of evil in the heavenly realms." (Ephesians 6:12)

My own sensing about Paul's language here is not only that there are spiritual forces behind much of the degradation of our societies. There are subhuman 'powers' and 'principalities' that

> *There are spiritual forces behind much of the degradation of our societies, subhuman 'powers' and 'principalities' that need to be confronted*

need to be confronted; life systems and structures that entrench the demonic, causing the defeat of well-meaning efforts and crushing the individuals that dare to transform them. Previous studies, like that of Walter Wink, have dealt in depth with the theological meaning of these 'powers'. For our present purpose, it is enough that the passage gives us a handle on why, sociologically, human institutions tend to develop internal contradictions and end up becoming the very opposite of what they set out to be.

Subjective change in inner attitudes towards social status, wealth creation and wealth sharing needs to be accompanied by objective changes in economic and social relations.

In ancient Israel, this was supposed to happen through a periodic re-arrangement of structures like the Sabbath laws, particularly the Ju-bilee Year. On the fiftieth year the slaves are to be released, the debts cancelled, and ancestral lands redeemed and returned to the original owners (Leviticus 25). Those who suffer economic reversals within the 50-year cycle are to be given a new start, freed from generational ser-vitude and indebtedness, and once again in possession of their patri-mony and economic means. It is unfortunate that even in Israel, this law was never really implemented, such that by Isaiah's time, we see extreme poverty and concentration of wealth: "Woe to you who add house to house and join field to field, till no space is left and you live alone in the land." (Isaiah 5:8)

Can we end poverty? Travelling through Europe, I noticed banners emblazoned in churches, 'Make poverty history'. This is the tagline of the Micah Challenge, a global campaign with a two-fold aim: a) to deepen the engagement of Christians with the poor and b) hold gov-ernments accountable to fulfil their public promise to cut to half pov-erty levels in their countries by 2015. As someone living in a corner of the world where poverty looks like a never-ending wrong, I thought this was a bit too optimistic. It struck me, though, that such confi-dence is perhaps peculiar to Europe, and may spring from a history of having substantially reduced poverty, or at least, enough to make the poor invisible.

Scripture, it seems to me, is both optimistic and realistic about ending poverty. In the early years of Israel, when the nation was yet in its incipient form, Moses declared that "there should be no poor among you ... if only you fully obey the Lord your God and are careful to follow all these commands I am giving you today." (Deuteronomy 15:4-5)

Israel was to be a showcase of a nation who, because she was care-fully obedient to the laws of loving God and neighbour, should have eliminated at least absolute poverty. To the extent that other societies are similarly sensitive to God's demands for justice and equity, there should be no absolute destitution among them.

At the same time, the same passage tells us that "There will always be poor people in the land." This strand of thinking finds reinforcement in Jesus' famous remark that "The poor you will always have with you, but you will not always have me." (See Matthew 26:11, Mark 14:7)

Certainly, by some stroke of misfortune or a complex of reasons, some people will inevitably fall through the cracks. But far from encouraging fatalism, this fact is supposed to rouse people to compassion: "Therefore I command you to be openhanded toward your brothers and toward the poor and needy in the land." (Deuteronomy 15:11) By such generosity, coupled with structural safety nets, those on the margins should only be a fraction of the population in a normal society.

Four

Discipling the Nations

Introduction: Christianity in Asia

CHRISTIANITY, we are told, began in the East, and Christian missions have been in Asia for a long time. The gospel was brought to this continent in the first century by missionaries like the apostle Thomas, who is said to have founded the churches from where the Syrian and Mar Thoma Christians in India have descended.

Yet Asia is the one continent where Christianity has made relatively little impact. After two thousand years, only about 3 to 5 percent of Asia's vast population are Christians. With the exception of the Philippines, local cultures continue to be deeply rooted in Hinduism, Buddhism, Islam and their variants, religious traditions that rival Christianity in philosophical depth.

What accounts for this inability to penetrate the cultures of Asia with the gospel?

The reasons behind this are many and complex, and would take a much longer analysis than we have time to do now. But perhaps a large part could be accounted to the continuing lack of a deep enough engagement with these great cultures.

Mission, as we know it today, originated from countries that came with the cross and the sword. In countries that are particularly resistant, Christianity is seen as a colonial religion. Its converts are considered to be no longer part of their cultures, aliens in their own land. This is particularly true in places like India or Japan.

The tiny churches in a large sea of local culture, are all too conscious that they are minorities and so feel besieged. This tends to result in further alienation. They drop out of the common life and retreat to their own self-enclosed spaces.

In countries where Christians are in the majority, or at least are not restricted by the government nor threatened by the dominant religious culture, the churches tend to be made in the image of the West. They take on the character of the sending missions, inheriting lock, stock and barrel their theological and ecclesiastical traditions. The Philippines is a good example. Influenced at first by Spanish Catholicism and later by American Protestantism, Filipino churches tend to be either suffused in mystic ritualism and sensuous imagery, or locked in cold intellectualism and an austere pietism. The gospel is understood to be merely for the 'soul', a legacy of Greek dualism that sees the body as a mere tomb for the spirit, and divides life between the sacred and the secular. Religion has to do only with the supernatural, with the appeasing of spirits through rituals and sacrifices, or with 'salvation', understood as merely getting a ticket to heaven or the assurance that 'all is well with my soul.'

Such retreat from everyday life has given the impression that the gospel has nothing to do with the structures that shape our societies. It continues to serve as a stumbling block to addressing poverty, the environment, governance and other such issues deemed 'worldly.' Our involvement in society has been limited to being peaceable citizens who pay taxes and do not 'rock the boat', so to speak.

The failure to engage cultures, to speak against sin as it expresses itself in institutions such as the caste system and other forms of systemic injustice, has meant the continuing irrelevance of the kind of Christianity that has been transplanted in Asia. As a consequence, the nations remain unreached, undiscipled in those aspects where they are most in need of conversion.

Rethinking the Great Commission
Matthew 28:16-20

W<small>E</small> are familiar with the idea of discipling individuals, of making Christ known and obeyed by people. We are less familiar, in fact may even be surprised, with the idea that we are to 'disciple nations.' But this is in fact the exact literal rendering of the original text of the Great Commission.

We are to disciple, not just individuals, but nations. So what exactly does this mean?

Our confidence

"All authority in heaven and on earth has been given to me ..." v. 18

Jesus appears to the disciples on a mountain in Galilee. There he inspires worship as well as doubt. We do not know exactly why some doubted. It is possible that some were still in the sort of state that made them cower in fear in the upper room. It may also be that they still could not make out what exactly has appeared before them. Is it a ghost? Has he really risen? And if he has, is it really him who stands before them? It seems that the risen Jesus had a body that is able to appear and disappear, and yet could be touched and handled. He was not just a spirit, but a living person who, while recognizable, had something richly strange about him.

Jesus speaks to this momentary confusion and doubt by saying that all power and authority had been given to him. He may have died in humiliation, but now he is alive and reigns supreme over all conceivable powers in all possible realms. He is king, and the kingdom has begun. There is a new element in human history. Jesus announces a new kind of existence where, because he reigns, we can cast out fear and all that hinders us from having a truly human life. We can have confidence because it is he who sits upon the throne.

Our commission

"Therefore as you go, make disciples of all nations ..." v.19

Scholars tell us that this verse is best translated, **"going, make disciples..."** or **"as you go, make disciples..."** The main verb is the making of disciples, not the going. This has large implications on how we do our witness.

'As you go', as you do your work, sit on a bus, or hang around with friends and colleagues, you make disciples. It means, for one, that the task of making disciples is to be done primarily as one goes about the daily business of life. Whether we are stay-at-home housewives chatting with neighbours over the clothesline, or

> *We are to engage people in their contexts and help them to work out their faith within their cultures and societies*

globally mobile professionals on business, we are to constantly bear witness through the quality of our work and the love in our relationships.

Also, we are told to **make disciples, not just of individuals, but of nations**. This means that not only people but entire life-systems are to be turned towards Christ. We are to engage people in their contexts, help them to work out their faith within their cultures and societies. To call nations to 'turn from idols to the living God' means that the central structures—like governance, business and family life—are to be brought under Jesus' lordship, in line with the norms and purposes for which they were instituted in the first place.

The Great Commission is not just about saving souls, but about redeeming whole communities of people from the bondage of sin as it expresses itself in our institutions and other forms of organized life.

It means dethroning the powers—whether economic, political or cultural—which seek to set themselves up as gods in place of the Lord of the nations. No longer are the nations ruled by spiritual powers, such as those symbolically named as the 'prince of Persia' or the 'prince of Greece' in Daniel 9 and 10. The risen Jesus rules over all these principalities, and over all the nations they once held in thrall. Every knee shall now bow, and all peoples be made subject to Christ. This is what is meant by 'discipling the nations'.

It also means that believers are **to be baptized in the name of the Triune God.** They are to declare publicly through this rite of passage that they belong to God, who has created, redeemed and sanctified them. To be baptized into the name of the three-Person God is to come under the full subjection and ownership of him who has brought us into being, bought us by his own life and purifies us by his empowering grace.

To teach them, or literally, to 'learn' them to 'obey all I have commanded you' means that the believers catch what Jesus is about by imitating the example of the apostles. They follow after the Master by seeing and hearing what the apostles themselves are doing. The disciples are to be part of a visible community that lives by all that Jesus taught, in such a way that the church becomes a community of lifelong learners. They are not meant to remain babies always rehashing early memories of conversion, or stuck with elementary doctrines of the faith. They are to continually grow into the height and depth of what means to belong to Christ.

Our companion

"I am with you always, to the very end of the age." v.20

Lest we get overwhelmed by the enormity of the task given, Jesus assures his disciples that "I am with you always …" Whatever road we are travelling, Jesus goes with us. We may not be aware of it, like the disheartened disciples on the road to Emmaus. Yet his risen life has inaugurated a new kind of existence where he is ever-present. Through all our fear, loneliness and uncertainty, he is our *kasama*, our companion, the one who goes with us. It is a Presence that will not leave us till the end of the age.

Micah is a global network and movement of Christian organizations and individuals, committed to integral mission as expressed through their response in ministries including relief, rehabilitation, development, creation care, justice, and peacemaking.

Established in 2001, Micah now has over 720 members in 91 countries.

Our vision inspires us towards the realization of communities living life in all its fullness, free from extreme poverty, injustice or conflict. Grounded in the Gospel, and becoming agents of change in our communities, we work to do this in three ways:

- being a catalyst for transforming mission through the promotion of integral mission

- working as a movement towards a united response to advocating for poverty reduction, justice, equality, reconciliation, safety and well-being for all

- having fellowship as a network, providing a platform for shared learning, corporate reflection and action, and facilitation of an information provision hub

Our motivating call to action is captured in Micah 6:8:

What does the Lord require of you? To act justly, and to love mercy, and to walk humbly with your God.

Find us at http://www.micahglobal.org

Lightning Source UK Ltd.
Milton Keynes UK
UKOW06f1053131116

287468UK00016B/570/P